One Wonderf...
12 Contempora...

Jenny Pedigo & Helen Robinson with Sherilyn Mortensen

MW00442531

Landauer Publishing, LLC

One Wonderful Curve
12 Contemporary Quilts

Copyright © 2015 by Landauer Publishing, LLC
Projects Copyright © 2015
by Jenny Pedigo & Helen Robinson for Sew Kind of Wonderful
     with Sherilyn Mortensen

This book was designed, produced,
and published by Landauer Publishing, LLC
3100 101st Street, Urbandale, IA 50322
515/287/2144   800/557/2144   landauerpub.com

President/Publisher: Jeramy Lanigan Landauer
Editor: Jeri Simon
Art Director: Laurel Albright
Photographer: Sue Voegtlin

All rights reserved. No part of this book may be reproduced or
transmitted in any form by any means, electronic or mechanical,
including photocopying, recording, or by any information
storage and retrieval system without permission in writing
from the publisher with the exception that the publisher grants
permission to enlarge the template patterns in this book for
personal use only. The scanning, uploading and distribution
of this book or any part thereof, via the Internet or any other
means without permission from the publisher is illegal and
punishable by law. The publisher presents the information in this
book in good faith. No warranty is given, nor are
results guaranteed.

Library of Congress: 2015950556

ISBN 13: 978-1-935726-77-7
This book printed on acid-free paper.
Printed in United States

10-9-8-7-6-5-4-3-2-1

 FACEBOOK.COM/
LANDAUERPUBLISHING
 YOUTUBE.COM/
LANDAUERPUBLISHING
 PINTEREST.COM/
LANDAUERPUB

Contents

Introduction

After growing up in a close-knit family that included four sisters and two brothers, it was difficult when everyone moved to different parts of the country. While our biennial reunions are a chance to catch up and enjoy time together, it just isn't enough. Quilting and cooking are two things we sisters have in common, so when Jenny began Sew Kind of Wonderful in 2010 she wanted all the sisters to join in the fun. Secretly, she wanted us to spend more time together.

Jenny

Helen

One day Sherilyn, sister three, cut some black and white paper shapes using the Quick Curve Ruler©. She began laying them out in a variety of interesting, unique designs. We realized this one shape was amazing and we could create wonderful projects with it. *One Wonderful Curve* was born. Our biggest challenge with this book has been limiting it to 12 designs. We know you'll be designing your own unique quilts with this wonderful curve.

Sherilyn

You will need the Quick Curve Ruler© to complete the projects in this book.

Look for the Quick Curve Ruler© at your favorite quilt shop or visit Sewkindofwonderful.com for ordering information and ruler tutorials.

Techniques Quick Curve Ruler© (QCR)

CUTTING THE CURVES

Each project in the book uses the same basic curved shape. Be sure to follow the instructions carefully, referring to the Techniques section as needed. We suggest you practice cutting and piecing the curves using the steps provided before beginning a project.

1. Cut (1) 7" x 12" fabric rectangle and (1) 8" contrasting fabric square. This will give you enough pieces to practice making two blocks.
Note: When making several blocks for a project, you can stack a few pieces, right sides up, for cutting.

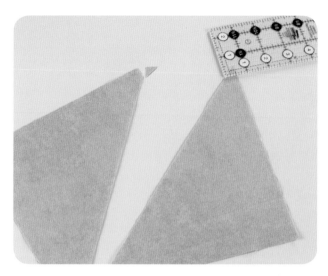

2. Cut the 8" contrasting fabric square in half diagonally. Measure in ½" on each point and trim.

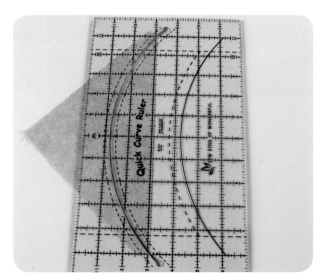

3. Position the QCR on the triangles with the curve cut out over the points as shown.

4. Using a 45mm rotary cutter, cut in the ruler's curve cut out to make a B shape. Discard the small piece.

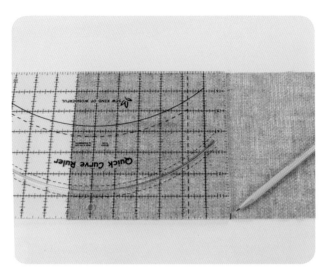

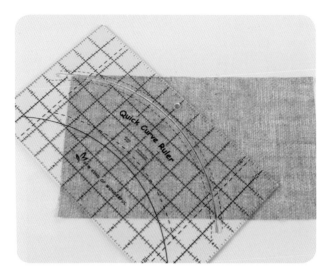

5. Place the 7" x 12" fabric rectangle right side up on a cutting surface. Measure and mark 7" on each long edge as shown.

6. Position the QCR on the rectangle with the ruler's curve cut out on the 7" mark and opposite corner.

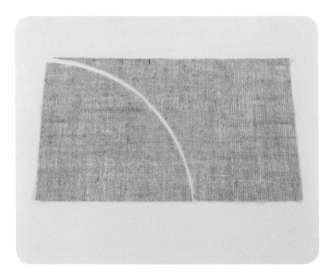

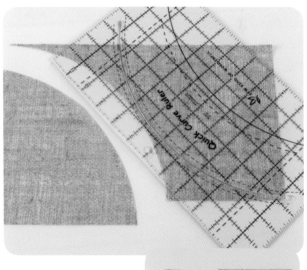

7. Using a 45mm rotary cutter, cut in the ruler's curve cut out to make an A shape.

8. Position the QCR on the remaining 7" mark and oppostie corner and cut to make an additional A shape. Discard the small center piece.

> TIP: Do not stack more than four fabric pieces when cutting.

Techniques Quick Curve Ruler© (QCR)

PIECING THE CURVES

The curves will be pieced in the same manner in each project. Always use a ¼" seam and sew with right sides together.

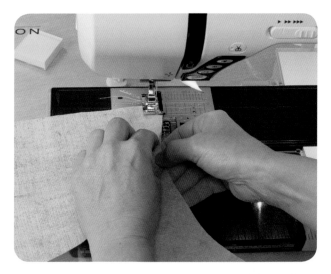

1. Position an A shape on a B shape, right sides together, with ½" of B extending beyond A.

2. Hold one shape in each hand and slowly bring the curved edges together while stitching a ¼" seam.

> TIP: When sewing the curves, I find it easiest to always have the outside curve (top piece) in my right hand and the inside curve (bottom piece) in my left hand. Experiment to see what works best for you.

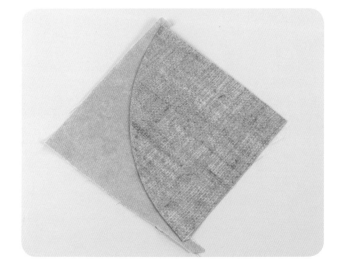

3. Press seam toward A to make an AB unit. Press the unit from the back and front.

SQUARING UP THE UNITS

Each project in the book will have its own specific set of Squaring Up the Units instructions. We suggest you practice squaring up the units made in Piecing the Curves on page 8 to practice.

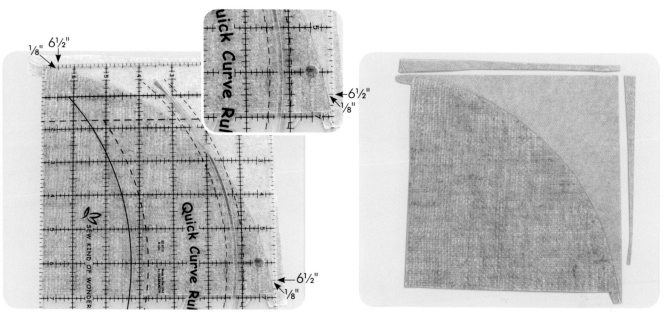

1. Square up the units made in Piecing the Curves to 6-$\frac{1}{2}$" square. Position the QCR on a unit with the 6-$\frac{1}{2}$" marks on the curved seam in the corners as shown. Leave an $\frac{1}{8}$" from curved seam to outer edge.

2. Trim the right and top edges of the unit.

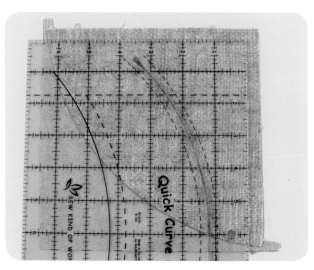

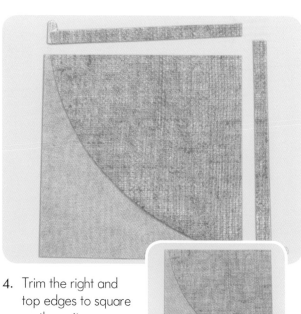

3. Lift the ruler and rotate the unit 180-degrees. Reposition the QCR on the unit so the previously trimmed edges are now on the 6-$\frac{1}{2}$" vertical and horizontal lines.

4. Trim the right and top edges to square up the unit.

Two color quilts have always been a favorite. I love quilting pearls and knew it would be a fun quilting element for this simple elegant runner. Since the citrine solid in Summer Citrus is a perfect match to my bedroom décor I use the runner on my bed, but as you can see it also makes a stunning table runner.

Finished size: 24" x 72"

Jenny

Summer Citrus Runner

MATERIALS

1-⅛ yards solid citrine fabric
1-⅛ yards solid white fabric
2-¼ yards backing fabric
½ yard binding fabric
Quick Curve Ruler©

GENERAL CUTTING INSTRUCTIONS

From solid citrine fabric, cut:
(5) 7-½" x WOF strips. From the strips, cut:
    (24) 7-½" squares

From solid white fabric, cut:
(5) 7-½" x WOF strips. From the strips, cut:
    (24) 7-½" squares

From binding fabric, cut:
(5) 2-½" x WOF binding strips

WOF = width of fabric
Read through Using the Quick Curve Ruler©
on pages 6-9 before beginning this project.

CUTTING WITH THE QUICK CURVE RULER©

1. Stack a few 7-½" solid citrine squares, right sides up. Measure and mark ½" on adjacent sides as shown.

2. Position the QCR on the fabric with the ruler's curve cut out on the ½" marks. Cut in the curve cut out with a rotary cutter to make A and B shapes as shown.

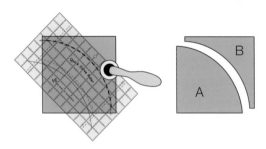

3. Repeat with the remaining 7-½" solid citrine and solid white squares to make a total of 48 A and B shapes.

Make 24

Make 24

4. Separate the A and B shapes into sets as shown.

11

PIECING THE CURVES

1. Referring to the diagram, position an A shape on a B shape, right sides together, with a ½" of B extending beyond A as shown.

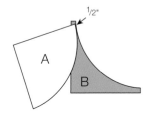

2. Hold one shape in each hand and slowly bring the curved edges together while stitching a ¼" seam. Press seam toward A to make an AB unit. Press the unit from the front and back. Repeat to make 24 AB units from each stack.

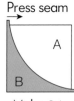 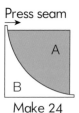

SQUARING UP THE AB UNITS

Square up the AB units to 6-½". Position the QCR on an AB unit with the 6-½" mark on the curved seam in the corners as shown. Leave an ⅛" from curved seam to outer edge. Trim the right and top edges of the unit. Lift the ruler and rotate the unit 180-degrees. Reposition the QCR on the unit so the previously trimmed edges are now on the 6-½" vertical and horizontal lines. Trim the right and top edges. Repeat with the remaining AB units.

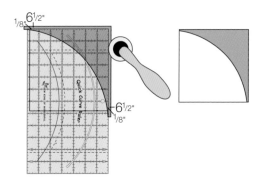

RUNNER ASSEMBLY

1. Referring to the Runner Assembly Diagram, lay out the AB units in 12 rows with 4 units in each row.

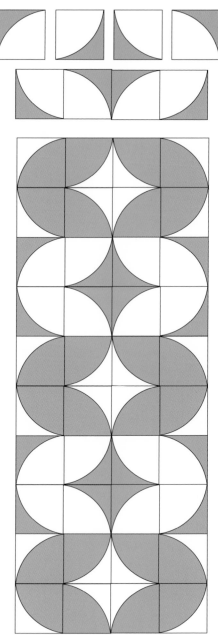

Runner Assembly Diagram

2. Sew the units together in rows. Press the seams. Sew the rows together to complete the runner top. Press.

FINISHING THE RUNNER

1. Layer the runner top, batting and backing together. Quilt as desired.

2. Sew the (5) 2-½" x WOF binding strips together to make one continuous strip. Press the strip in half lengthwise and sew the binding strip to the raw edge of the runner top. Fold the binding over raw edges and hand stitch in place on back of runner.

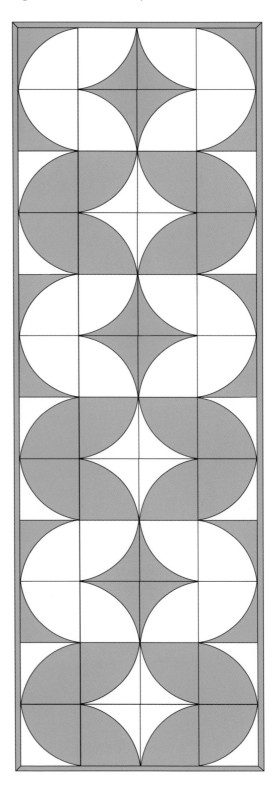

I love the simple design that gives a feel of movement to Contempo Twist. The never-ending twist of ribbons reminds me of the ribbon candy Granny always had during the holidays.

Sherilyn

Finished size: 60" x 60"

Contempo Twist Quilt

MATERIALS

2-½ yards solid red fabric
(4) ⅔ yard cuts assorted black/white print fabric
4 yards backing fabric
½ yard binding fabric
Quick Curve Ruler©

GENERAL CUTTING INSTRUCTIONS

From solid red fabric, cut:

(7) 7-½" x WOF strips. From the strips, cut:
  (32) 7-½" squares

(3) 12" x WOF strips. From the strips, cut:
  (14) 7" x 12" pieces

**From *each* black/white print fabric,
cut in this order:**

(2) 7-½" x WOF strips. From the strips, cut:
  (9) 7-½" squares for a total of 36 squares

(1) 8" x WOF strip. From the strip, cut:
  (3) 8" squares. Cut each in half diagonally for
  a total of 24 triangles
  (2) 6-½" squares

From binding fabric, cut:

(7) 2-½" x WOF binding strips

WOF = width of fabric
Read through Using the Quick Curve Ruler©
on pages 6-9 before beginning this project.

CUTTING WITH THE QUICK CURVE RULER©

1. Stack a few 7-½" solid red squares, right sides up.
   Measure and mark ½" on adjacent sides as shown.

2. Position the QCR on the fabric with the ruler's
   curve cut out on the ½" marks. Cut in the curve
   cut out with a rotary cutter to make A and B
   shapes as shown.

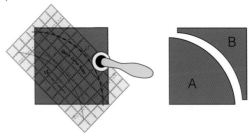

3. Repeat with the remaining 7-½" solid red and black/
   white print squares to make a total of 68 A and B
   shapes. Set aside 4 black/white A shapes. You will
   only use 32.

Make 32   Make 36

4. Stack a few 7" x 12" solid red pieces, right sides up.
   Measure and mark 7" on each long edge as shown.
   Position the QCR on the fabric with the ruler's curve
   cut out on the 7" mark and opposite corner. Cut in
   the curve cut out to make an A shape.

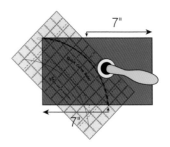

5. In the same manner, position the QCR on the remaining 7" mark and cut to make another A shape. Discard small piece in center. Repeat with the remaining 7" x 12" solid red pieces for a total of 28 red A shapes.

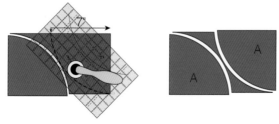

6. Stack a few 8" black/white print triangles together, right sides up. Measure in ½" on both points and trim as shown.

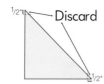

7. Position the QCR on the triangles with the curve cut out over the points as shown. Using a rotary cutter, cut in the curve cut out to make a B shape. Discard the small pieces. Repeat with the remaining 8" black/white print triangles for a total of 24 black/white print B shapes.

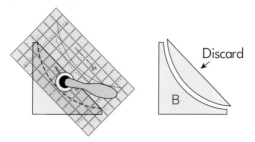

PIECING THE CURVES

1. Separate the A and B shapes into sets as shown.

2. Referring to the diagram, position a solid red A shape on a black/white print B shape, right sides together, with a ½" of B extending beyond A.

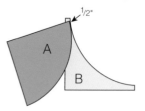

3. Hold one shape in each hand and slowly bring the curved edges together while stitching a ¼" seam. Press seam toward A to make an AB unit. Press the unit from the front and back.

4. Repeat with the remaining A and B shapes to make a total of 92 AB units.

Make 60   Make 32

SQUARING UP THE AB UNITS

Square up the AB units to 6-½". Position the QCR on an AB unit with the 6-½" mark on the curved seam in the corners as shown. Leave an ⅛" from curved seam to outer edge. Trim the right and top edges of the unit. Lift the ruler and rotate the unit 180-degrees. Reposition the QCR on the unit so the previously trimmed edges are now on the 6-½" vertical and horizontal lines. Trim the right and top edges. Repeat with the remaining AB units.

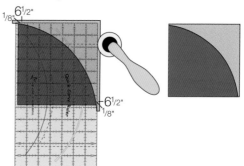

MAKING THE CONTEMPO TWIST QUADRANTS

Note: This quilt has a directional layout that can be divided into 4 quadrants. To aid in lay out and assembly sew one quadrant together at a time.

1. Lay out 23 AB units and (2) 6-½" black/white print squares as shown. Sew the pieces together in rows. Press the seams.

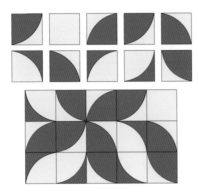

2. Sew the rows together to complete the quadrant. Press. Place a safety pin in the top left corner of the quadrant. Repeat to make a total of four quadrants, placing a safety pin in the top left corner of each quadrant.

Make 4 Quadrants

Quilt Assembly Diagram

QUILT ASSEMBLY

1. Referring to the Quilt Assembly Diagram, lay out the 4 quadrants with the four pinned blocks in the four corners of the quilt as shown.

2. Sew the quadrants together in rows. Press seams. Sew the rows together. Press seams.

FINISHING THE QUILT

1. Layer the quilt top, batting and backing together. Quilt as desired.

2. Sew the (7) 2-½" x WOF binding strips together to make one continuous strip. Press the strip in half lengthwise and sew the binding strip to the raw edge of the quilt top. Fold binding over raw edges and hand stitch in place on back of quilt.

The Churn Dash block has always been one of my favorite traditional blocks. Mod Dash evolved after many failed attempts and lots of sisterly collaboration. We love the balance and symmetry of this design with the center block balancing the negative spaces.

Jenny

Finished size: 48" x 48"

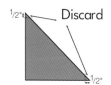

Mod Dash Quilt

MATERIALS

1 yard dark orange fabric
½ yard orange 1 fabric
½ yard orange 2 fabric
½ yard orange 3 fabric
¾ yard white fabric
2 yards gray background fabric
3 yards backing fabric
⅜ yard binding fabric
Quick Curve Ruler© (QCR)

GENERAL CUTTING INSTRUCTIONS

From dark orange fabric, cut:
(2) 7" x 12" pieces

(4) 4" x 12-½" pieces

From *each* orange fabric (including dark orange), cut:
(2) 8" x WOF strips. From each strip, cut:
   (3) 8" squares. Cut each in half diagonally to make 48 triangles

(1) 2-½" square

From white fabric, cut:
(1) 8" x WOF strip. From the strip, cut:
   (4) 8" squares. Cut each in half diagonally to make 8 triangles

(4) 3" x 12-½" pieces

(3) 2-½" x WOF strips. From the strips, cut:
   (48) 2-½" squares

From gray background fabric, cut:
(9) 7" x WOF strips. From the strips, cut:
   (26) 7" x 12" pieces

From binding fabric, cut:
(5) 2-½" x WOF binding strips

WOF = width of fabric
Read through Using the Quick Curve Ruler©
on pages 6-9 before beginning this project.

CUTTING WITH THE QUICK CURVE RULER©

1. Stack a few 8" orange triangles together, right sides up. Measure in ½" on both points and trim as shown.

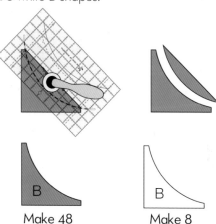

2. Position the QCR on the triangles with the curve cut out over the points as shown. Using a rotary cutter, cut in the curve cut out to make a B shape. Discard small section. Repeat with the remaining 8" orange and white triangles to make a total of 48 orange and 8 white B shapes.

Make 48   Make 8

3. Stack a few 7" x 12" gray background pieces together, right sides up. Measure and mark 7" on each long edge as shown. Position the QCR on the fabric with the ruler's curve cut out on the 7" mark and opposite corner. Cut in curve cut out to make an A shape.

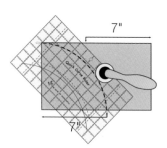

4. In the same manner, position the QCR on the remaining 7" mark and cut to make another A shape. Discard small piece in center. Repeat with the remaining 7" x 12" gray background and dark orange pieces for a total of 52 gray A shapes and 4 dark orange A shapes.

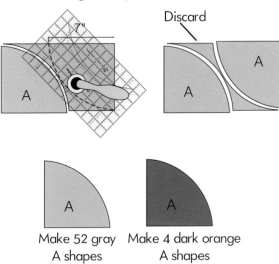

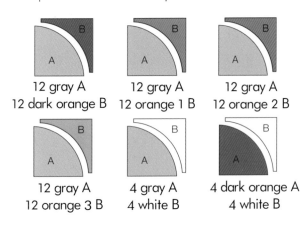

Make 52 gray A shapes   Make 4 dark orange A shapes

PIECING THE CURVES

1. Separate the A and B shapes into sets as shown.

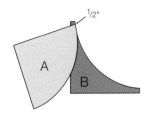

| 12 gray A | 12 gray A | 12 gray A |
| 12 dark orange B | 12 orange 1 B | 12 orange 2 B |

| 12 gray A | 4 gray A | 4 dark orange A |
| 12 orange 3 B | 4 white B | 4 white B |

2. Referring to the diagram, position an A shape on a B shape, right sides together, with a ½" of B extending beyond A.

3. Hold one shape in each hand and slowly bring the curved edges together while stitching a ¼" seam. Press seam toward A to make an AB unit. Press the unit from the front and back.

Press seam

4. Repeat with the remaining A and B shapes to make a total of 56 AB units.

Make 56 AB units

SQUARING UP THE AB UNITS

Square up the AB units to 6-½". Position the QCR on an AB unit with the 6-½" mark on the curved seam in the corners as shown. Leave an ⅛" from curved seam to outer edge. Trim the right and top edges of the unit. Lift the ruler and rotate the unit 180-degrees. Reposition the QCR on the unit so the previously trimmed edges are now on the 6-½" vertical and horizontal lines. Trim the right and top edges. Repeat with the remaining AB units.

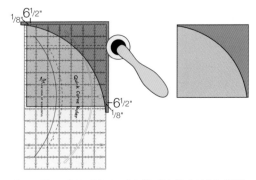

MAKING THE MOD DIAMOND BLOCK UNITS

1. Draw a diagonal line on the wrong side of the white 2-½" squares. Position a marked square on a corner of a gray/orange AB unit, right sides together, as shown.

2. Stitch on the drawn line. Trim fabric ¼" past the stitched line. Press seam open. Repeat with remaining gray/orange AB units to make a total of 48 gray/orange units.

Make 48
gray/orange units

3. Draw a diagonal line on the wrong side of the assorted orange 2-½" squares. Position a marked square on a corner of a gray/white AB unit, right sides together, as shown.

4. Stitch on the drawn line. Trim fabric ¼" past the stitched line. Press seam open. Repeat with remaining gray/white AB units to make a total of 4 gray/white units.

Make 4
gray/white units

MAKING THE MOD DIAMOND BLOCKS

1. Lay out 4 orange/gray units as shown. There should be one of each orange colorway.

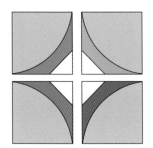

2. Sew the units together in rows. Sew the rows together to complete a mod diamond block. Press. Repeat to make a total of 12 mod diamond blocks.

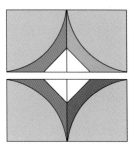 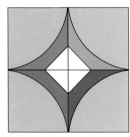

Make 12 Mod
Diamond Blocks

MAKING THE CHURN DASH BLOCK

1. Sew a 3" x 12-½" white piece to a 4" x 12-½" dark orange piece as shown. Press. Repeat to make 4 white/orange sets.

Make 4
white/orange sets

2. Lay out 4 white/gray units as shown. Sew the units together in rows. Sew the rows together to complete a center diamond block. Press.

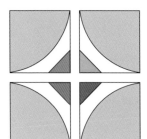 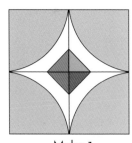

Make 1
Center Diamond Block

CHURN DASH BLOCK ASSEMBLY

Referring to the center block diagram, lay out the center diamond block, white/orange sets and dark orange/white AB units in rows as shown. Sew the pieces together in rows to complete the churn dash block.

Churn Dash Block Diagram

QUILT ASSEMBLY

1. Lay out 4 mod diamond blocks and the churn dash block as shown. Sew the mod diamond blocks together in pairs. Press.

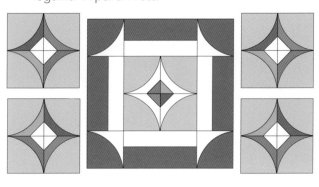

2. Sew block pairs to the churn dash block as shown. Press.

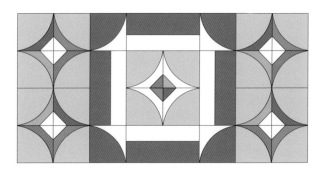

3. Lay out the remaining 8 mod diamond blocks and churn dash section together as shown.

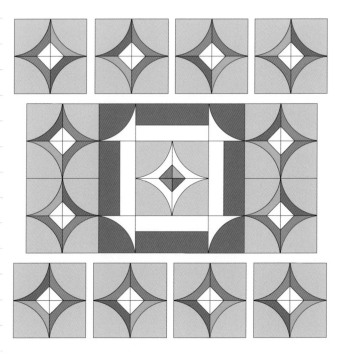

4. Sew the blocks together in rows.

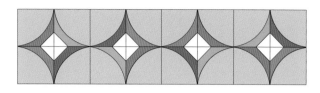

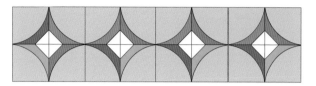

5. Sew the rows to the center section to complete the quilt top. Press.

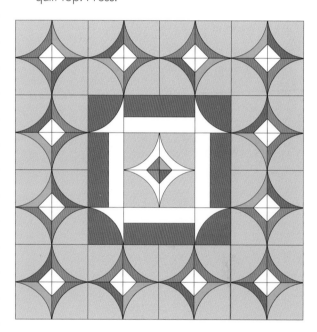

FINISHING THE QUILT

1. Layer the quilt top, batting and backing together. Quilt as desired.

2. Sew the (5) 2-½" x WOF binding strips together to make one continuous strip. Press the strip in half lengthwise and sew the binding strip to the raw edge of the quilt top. Fold binding over raw edges and hand stitch in place on back of quilt.

Candy Blossoms is the best of all three of us. Jenny chose the fabrics, Sherilyn pieced the top and I quilted it. It is a great example of our sisterly bond and how well we work together to create something more beautiful than any one of us could have done alone.

Helen

Finished size: 80" x 102"

Candy Blossoms Quilt

MATERIALS

(15) ½ yard cuts assorted prints
1-¼ yards solid gray fabric
¾ yard solid violet fabric
¾ yard solid gold fabric
5-½ yards tan background fabric
⅔ yard binding fabric
8 yards backing fabric
Quick Curve Ruler© (QCR)

GENERAL CUTTING INSTRUCTIONS

From *each* assorted print, cut:
(2) 7-½" x WOF strips. From the strips, cut:
   (10) 7-½" squares for a total of 150 squares.
   You will only use 144.

From solid gray fabric, cut:
(5) 8" x WOF strips. From the strips, cut:
   (24) 8" squares. Cut each in half
   diagonally to make 48 triangles

From solid violet fabric, cut:
(3) 8" x WOF strips. From the strips, cut:
   (12) 8" squares. Cut each in half
   diagonally to make 24 triangles

From solid gold fabric, cut:
(3) 8" x WOF strips. From the strips, cut:
   (12) 8" squares. Cut each in half
   diagonally to make 24 triangles

From tan background fabric, cut:
(10) 8" x WOF strips. From the strips, cut:
   (48) 8" squares. Cut each in half
   diagonally to make 96 triangles

(8) 7" x WOF strips. From the strips, cut:
   (24) 7" x 12" pieces

(20) 2-½" x WOF strips. Sew the strips together
   end to end to make one strip.
   From the strip, cut:
   (8) 2-½" x 24-½" sashing pieces
   (3) 2-½" x 76-½" sashing pieces
   (2) 2-½" x 102-½" border pieces
   (2) 2-½" x 80-½" border pieces

From binding fabric, cut:
(10) 2-½" x WOF binding strips

WOF = width of fabric
Read through Using the Quick Curve Ruler©
on pages 6-9 before beginning this project.

MAKING THE HALF-SQUARE TRIANGLE UNITS

1. Choose two 7-½" assorted print squares. Draw a diagonal line on the wrong side of one of the squares.

2. Layer the two squares, right sides together, with the marked square on top. Sew ¼" on both sides of the drawn line.

3. Cut on the drawn line. Press open to make 2 half-square triangle units.

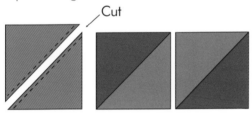

4. Repeat with the remaining assorted print squares to make 144 half-square triangle units.

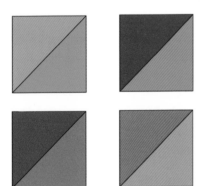

Make 144 half-square triangle units

CUTTING WITH THE QUICK CURVE RULER©

1. Stack a few half-square triangle units, right sides up. Measure and mark 7" on adjacent sides as shown.

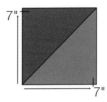

2. Position the QCR on the unit with the ruler's curve cut out on the 7" marks. Cut in the curve cut out with a rotary cutter to make an A shape as shown.

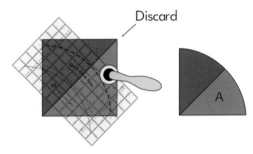

3. Repeat with the remaining half-square triangle units to make a total of 144 A shapes.

4. Stack a few 8" tan background half-square triangles together, right sides up. Measure in ½" on both points and trim as shown.

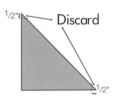

5. Position the QCR on the half-square triangles with the curve cut out over the points as shown. Using a rotary cutter, cut in the curve cut out to make a B shape. Discard the small pieces.

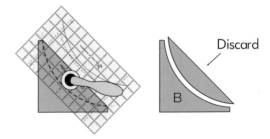

6. Repeat with the remaining 8" tan background, gold, violet and gray half-square triangles to make the number shown in the diagram.

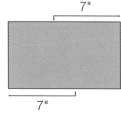

| Make 24 | Make 24 | Make 48 | Make 96 |

7. Stack a few 7" x 12" tan background pieces. Measure and mark 7" on each long edge as shown.

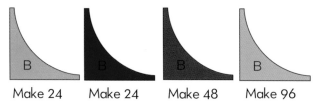

8. Position the QCR on the fabric with the ruler's curve cut out on the 7" mark and opposite corner. Cut in the curve cut out to make an A shape as shown.

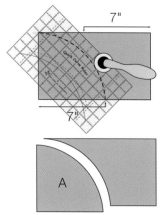

9. In the same manner, position the QCR on the remaining 7" mark and cut to make another A shape. Discard small piece in center. Repeat with the remaining 7" x 12" tan background pieces to make a total of 48 A shapes.

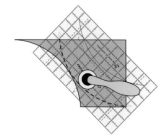

Make 48

PIECING THE CURVES

1. Separate the A and B shapes into sets as shown.

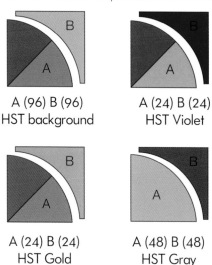

A (96) B (96)
HST background

A (24) B (24)
HST Violet

A (24) B (24)
HST Gold

A (48) B (48)
HST Gray

2. Referring to the diagram, position an A shape on a B shape, right sides together, with a ½" of B extending beyond A.

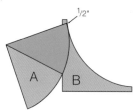

3. Hold one shape in each hand and slowly bring the curved edges together while stitching a ¼" seam. Press seam toward A to make an AB unit. Press the unit from the front and back.

4. Repeat with the remaining A and B shapes to make a total of 192 AB units.

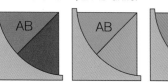

Make 192 AB units

SQUARING UP THE AB UNITS

Square up the AB units to 6-½". Position the QCR on an AB unit with the 6-½" mark on the curved seam in the corners as shown. Leave an 1/8" from curved seam to outer edge. Trim the right and top edges of the unit. Lift the ruler and rotate the unit 180-degrees. Reposition the QCR on the unit so the previously trimmed edges are now on the 6-½" vertical and horizontal lines. Trim the right and top edges. Repeat with the remaining AB units.

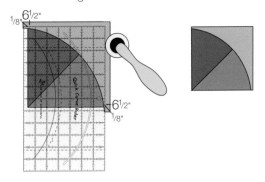

MAKING THE CANDY BLOSSOM BLOCK

1. Lay out (16) AB units in 4 rows with 4 units in each row as shown.

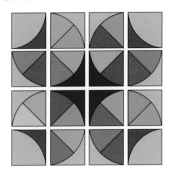

2. Sew the pieces together in rows. Sew the rows together to make a candy blossom block with a violet center. Make a total of 6 violet center candy blossom blocks. Repeat to make 6 gold center candy blossom blocks.

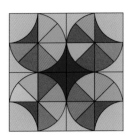

Make 6

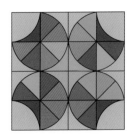

Make 6

QUILT ASSEMBLY

1. Referring to the Row Assembly Diagram, lay out the candy blossom blocks and 2-½" x 24-½" sashing pieces together in rows as shown.

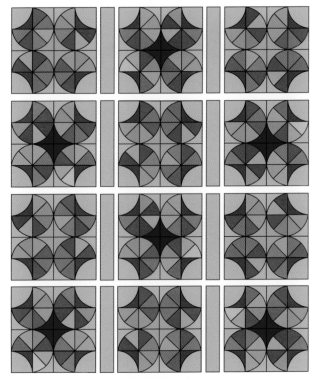

Row Assembly Diagram

2. Sew the pieces together in rows. Press seams toward the sashing

3. Lay out the 4 block rows and 2-$\frac{1}{2}$" x 76-$\frac{1}{2}$" sashing pieces as shown. Sew the pieces together. Press seams toward the sashing to complete the quilt center.

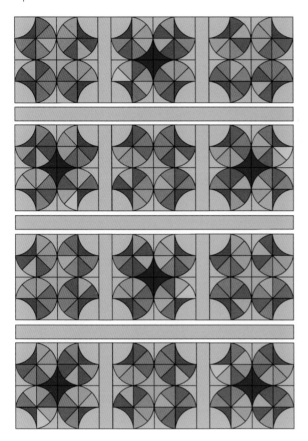

4. Sew the 2-$\frac{1}{2}$" x 102-$\frac{1}{2}$" border pieces to opposite sides of the quilt center. Press seams toward the border. Sew the 2-$\frac{1}{2}$" x 80-$\frac{1}{2}$" border pieces to the top and bottom of the quilt center. Press seams toward the border.

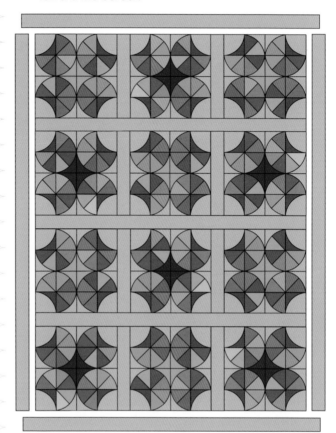

FINISHING THE QUILT

1. Layer the quilt top, batting and backing together. Quilt as desired.

2. Sew the (10) 2-$\frac{1}{2}$" x WOF binding strips together to make one continuous strip. Press the strip in half lengthwise and sew the binding strip to the raw edge of the quilt top. Fold binding over raw edges and hand stitch in place on back of quilt.

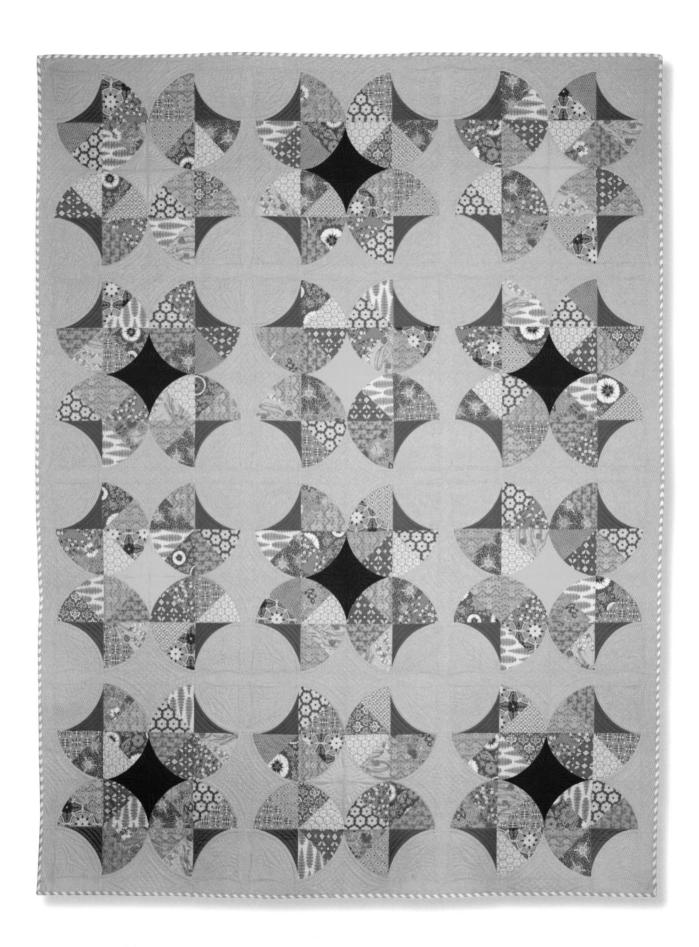

Gaggle Battle uses a simple traditional block. I gave it a fresh look with a fun layout and just the slightest curve to add interest and motion. Denyse Schmidt designs some of my favorite fabrics and I used her Franklin line in this quilt.

Jenny

Finished size: 72" x 84"

Gaggle Battle Quilt

MATERIALS

(7) ½ yard cuts assorted prints

¾ yard coordinating solid fabric

Note: We used 2 coordinating solids in the featured quilt.

5-½ yards white background fabric

5-¼ yards backing fabric

⅔ yard binding fabric

Quick Curve Ruler© (QCR)

GENERAL CUTTING INSTRUCTIONS

From *each* assorted print, cut:

(2) 8" x WOF strips. From the strips, cut:
  (10) 8" squares. Cut each in half diagonally to make a total of 140 triangles

From coordinating solid fabric, cut:

(3) 8" x WOF strips. From the strips, cut:
  (14) 8" squares. Cut each in half diagonally to make 28 triangles

From white background fabric, cut:

(28) 7" x WOF strips. From the strips, cut:
  (84) 7" x 12" pieces

From binding fabric, cut:

(9) 2-½" x WOF binding strips

WOF = width of fabric

Read through Using the Quick Curve Ruler© on pages 6-9 before beginning this project.

CUTTING WITH QUICK CURVE RULER©

1. Stack a few 8" assorted print triangles, right sides up. Measure in ½" on both points and trim as shown.

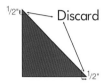

2. Position the QCR on the triangles with the ruler's curve cut out on the ½" marks. Cut in the curve cut out with a rotary cutter to make B shapes as shown.

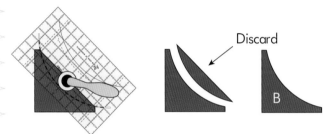

3. Repeat with the remaining 8" assorted prints and coordinating solid triangles.

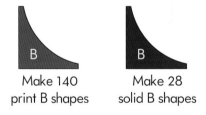

Make 140
print B shapes

Make 28
solid B shapes

4. Stack a few 7" x 12" white background pieces, right sides up. Measure and mark 7" on each long edge as shown. Position the QCR on the fabric with the ruler's curve cut out on the 7" mark and opposite corner. Cut in the curve cut out to make an A shape as shown.

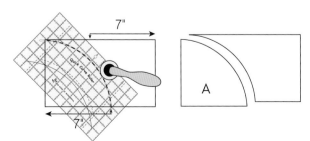

5. In the same manner, position the QCR on the remaining 7" mark and cut to make another A shape. Discard small piece in center. Repeat with the remaining 7" x 12" white background pieces for a total of 168 A shapes.

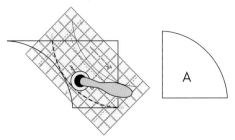

Note: You should have (20) B shapes of each assorted print, (28) B shapes of coordinating solid and (168) A shapes white background fabric.

PIECING THE CURVES

1. Separate the A and B shapes into sets as shown.

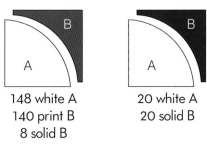

148 white A
140 print B
8 solid B

20 white A
20 solid B

2. Referring to the diagram, position an A shape on a B shape, right sides together, with a ½" of B extending beyond A.

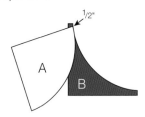

3. Hold one shape in each hand and slowly bring the curved edges together while stitching a ¼" seam. Press seam toward A to make an AB unit. Press the unit from the front and back.

Press seam

4. Repeat with the remaining A and B shapes to make a total of 168 AB units.

Make 168 AB units

SQUARING UP THE AB UNITS

Square up the AB units to 6-½". Position the QCR on an AB unit with the 6-½" mark on the curved seam in the corners as shown. Leave an ⅛" from curved seam to outer edge. Trim the right and top edges of the unit. Lift the ruler and rotate the unit 180-degrees. Reposition the QCR on the unit so the previously trimmed edges are now on the 6-½" vertical and horizontal lines. Trim the right and top edges. Repeat with the remaining AB units.

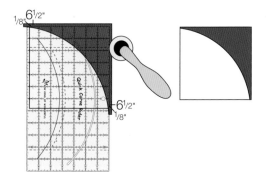

QUILT ASSEMBLY

1. Referring to the Quilt Assembly Diagram, lay out the AB units in 14 rows with 12 units in each.

2. Sew the units together in rows. Press seams. Sew the rows together to complete the quilt top. Press seams.

Quilt Assembly Diagram

FINISHING THE QUILT

1. Layer the quilt top, batting and backing together. Quilt as desired.

2. Sew the (9) 2-½" x WOF binding strips together to make one continuous strip. Press the strip in half lengthwise and sew the binding strip to the raw edge of the quilt top. Fold binding over raw edges and hand stitch in place on back of quilt.

The curves created with the Quick Curve Ruler® have always reminded us of the Middle East and its iconic curved dome buildings. Moroccan Vibe has a variety of layout options —a long runner or a runner with each large block rotated a quarter turn.

Helen

Finished size: 48" x 48"

Moroccan Vibe Quilt

MATERIALS

8 fat quarters assorted prints
1 fat quarter for block centers
2 yards white background fabric
$\frac{1}{2}$ yard dark solid fabric
$\frac{2}{3}$ yard binding fabric
3-$\frac{1}{2}$ yards backing fabric
Quick Curve Ruler© (QCR)

GENERAL CUTTING INSTRUCTIONS

 From *each* assorted fat quarter, cut as shown:
(1) 7" C square

(1) 8" square. Cut each in
    half diagonally
    to make 16 triangles

(2) 7-$\frac{1}{2}$" squares

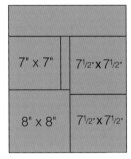

From block center fat quarter, cut:
(16) 4" squares

From white background fabric, cut:
(6) 7" x WOF strips. From the strips, cut:
    (16) 7" x 12" pieces

(2) 8" x WOF strips. From the strips, cut:
    (8) 8" squares. Cut each in half diagonally to
    make 16 triangles

From dark solid fabric, cut:
(2) 7" x WOF strips. From the strips, cut:
    (8) 7" D squares

From binding fabric, cut:
(6) 2-$\frac{1}{2}$" x WOF binding strips

WOF = width of fabric
Read through Using the Quick Curve Ruler©
on pages 6-9 before beginning this project.

CUTTING WITH QUICK CURVE RULER©

1. Stack a few 7-$\frac{1}{2}$" assorted print squares, right
   sides up. Measure and mark $\frac{1}{2}$" on adjacent sides
   as shown.

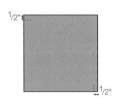

2. Position the QCR on the squares with the ruler's
   curve cut out on the $\frac{1}{2}$" marks. Cut in the curve
   cut out with a rotary cutter to make A and B shapes
   as shown.

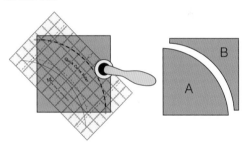

3. Repeat with the remaining 7-$\frac{1}{2}$" assorted print
   squares to make a total of 16 A and 16 B shapes.

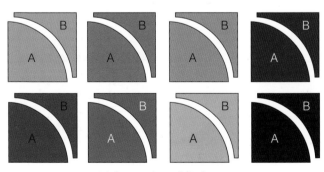

Make 16 A and B shapes
(2 from each print)

4. Stack a few 8" white background triangles, right sides up. Measure in ½" on both points and trim as shown.

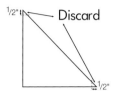

5. Position the QCR on the triangles with the ruler's curve cut out on the ½" marks. Cut in the curve cut out with a rotary cutter to make B shapes as shown.

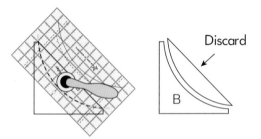

6. Repeat with the remaining 8" white background and assorted print triangles to make a total of 16 white B and 16 assorted print B shapes.

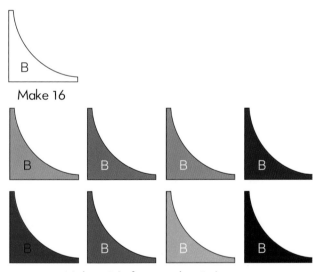

Make 16

Make 16 (2 from each print)

7. Stack a few 7" x 12" white background pieces, right sides up. Measure and mark 7" on each long edge as shown.

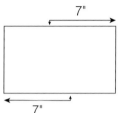

8. Position the QCR on the fabric with the ruler's curve cut out on the 7" mark and opposite corner. Cut in the curve cut out to make an A shape as shown.

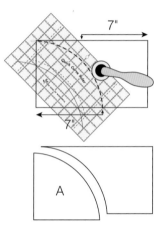

9. In the same manner, position the QCR on the remaining 7" mark and cut to make another A shape. Discard small piece in center. Repeat with the remaining 7" x 12" white background pieces to make a total of 32 A shapes.

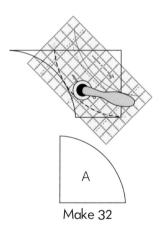

Make 32

PIECING THE CURVES

1. Separate the A and B shapes into sets as shown.

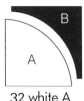

32 white A
32 print B

16 print A
16 white B

2. Referring to the diagram, position an A shape on a B shape, right sides together, with a ½" of B extending beyond A.

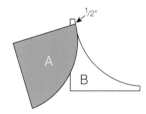

3. Hold one shape in each hand and slowly bring the curved edges together while stitching a ¼" seam. Press seam toward A to make an AB unit. Press the unit from the front and back.

Press seam

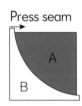

4. Repeat with the remaining A and B shapes to make a total of 48 AB units.

Make 48 AB units

SQUARING UP THE AB UNITS

Square up the AB units to 6-½". Position the QCR on an AB unit with the 6-½" mark on the curved seam in the corners as shown. Leave an ⅛" from curved seam to outer edge. Trim the right and top edges of the unit. Lift the ruler and rotate the unit 180-degrees. Reposition the QCR on the unit so the previously trimmed edges are now on the 6-½" vertical and horizontal lines. Trim the right and top edges. Repeat with the remaining AB units.

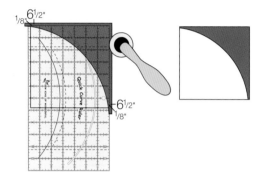

MAKING THE CENTER BLOCK UNITS

1. Draw a diagonal line on the wrong side of the 7" dark solid D squares as shown.

2. Layer the marked square on a 7" assorted print C square, right sides together, with the marked square on top. Sew ¼" on both sides of the drawn line.

3. Cut on the drawn line. Press open to make 2 half-square triangle units. Square the units to 6-½".

Cut

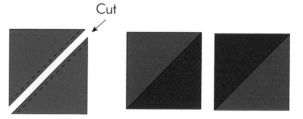

4. Repeat with the remaining 7" dark solid and assorted print C and D squares to make 16 half-square triangle units.

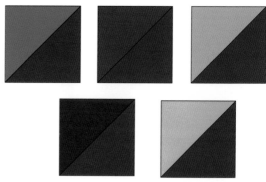

Make 16 half-square triangle units

5. Draw a diagonal line on the wrong side of the 4" block center squares as shown.

6. Position a marked 4" square on a dark corner of a half-square triangle unit, right sides together. Stitch on the drawn line.

7. Trim the corner fabric ¼" past the stitched line. Press seam open to make a center block unit. Repeat to make 16 center block units.

Make 16 center block units

MAKING THE MOROCCAN VIBE BLOCK

Note: Use two matching fabrics in each block.

1. Lay out 12 AB units and 4 center block units in 4 rows as shown. Sew the units together in rows. Press seams.

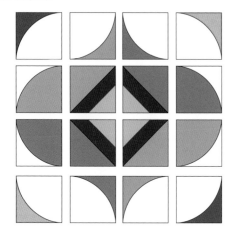

2. Sew the rows together to complete a Moroccan vibe block. Make a total of 4 Moroccan vibe blocks. Press seams.

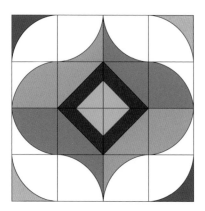

Make 4

QUILT ASSEMBLY

1. Referring to the Quilt Assembly Diagram, lay out 4 Moroccan vibe blocks as shown.

2. Sew the blocks together in rows. Sew the rows together to complete the quilt top. Press seams.

Quilt Assembly Diagram

FINISHING THE QUILT

1. Layer the quilt top, batting and backing together. Quilt as desired.

2. Sew the (6) 2-½" x WOF binding strips together to make one continuous strip. Press the strip in half lengthwise and sew the binding strip to the raw edge of the quilt top. Fold binding over raw edges and hand stitch in place on back of quilt.

I love the modern feel of Persimmon. The fresh orange and white colors remind me of cool Creamcicle® pops. The pattern is simple yet the design is intricate and pleasing .

Sherilyn

Finished size: 74" x 74"

Persimmon Quilt

MATERIALS

1-⅔ yards solid orange fabric
4-½ yards solid white fabric
5 yards backing fabric
⅔ yard binding fabric
Quick Curve Ruler© (QCR)

GENERAL CUTTING INSTRUCTIONS

From solid orange fabric, cut:
(4) 7-½" x WOF strips. From the strips, cut:
    (20) 7-½" squares

(2) 12" x WOF strips. From the strips, cut:
    (10) 7" x 12" pieces

From solid white fabric, cut in the following order:
(4) 24-½" x WOF strips. From the strips, cut:
    (4) 24-½" squares
    From left-over fabric from strips, cut:
    (20) 7-½" squares

(2) 8" x WOF strips. From the strips, cut:
    (10) 8" squares. Cut each in half diagonally
    to make 20 triangles

(8) 1-½" x WOF strips. Sew the strips together
    end to end and cut:
    (2) 1-½" x 72-½" borders
    (2) 1-½" x 74-½" borders

(4) 6-½" x WOF strips. From the strips, cut:
    (20) 6-½" squares

From binding fabric, cut:
(8) 2-½" x WOF binding strips

WOF = width of fabric
Read through *Using the Quick Curve Ruler©*
on pages 6-9 before beginning this project.

CUTTING WITH QUICK CURVE RULER©

1. Stack a few 7-½" solid orange squares, right sides up. Measure and mark ½" on adjacent sides as shown.

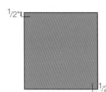

2. Position the QCR on the squares with the ruler's curve cut out on the ½" marks. Cut in the curve cut out with a rotary cutter to make A and B shapes as shown.

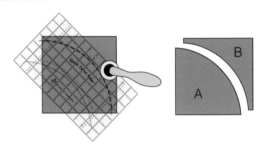

3. Repeat with the remaining 7-½" solid orange and solid white squares.

Make 20

Make 20

4. Stack a few 8" solid white triangles together, right sides up. Measure in ½" on both points and trim as shown.

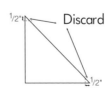

5. Position the QCR on the triangles with the curve cut out over the points as shown. Using a rotary cutter, cut in the curve cut out to make a B shape. Discard the small pieces. Repeat with the remaining 8" solid white triangles to make a total of 20 B shapes.

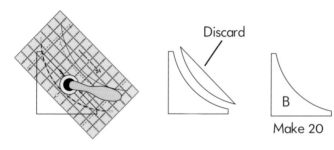

Discard

B

Make 20

6. Stack a few 7" x 12" solid orange pieces, right sides up. Measure and mark 7" on each long edge as shown. Position the QCR on the fabric with the ruler's curve cut out on the 7" mark and opposite corner. Cut in the curve cut out to make an A shape as shown.

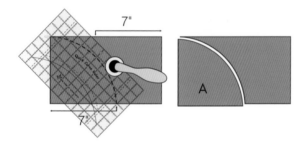

7"

7"

A

7. In the same manner, position the QCR on the remaining 7" mark and cut to make another A shape. Discard small piece in center. Repeat with the remaining 7" x 12" solid orange pieces to make a total of 20 A shapes.

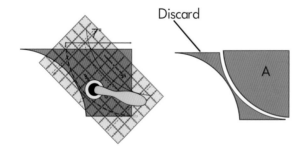

Discard

A

PIECING THE CURVES

1. Separate the A and B shapes into sets as shown.

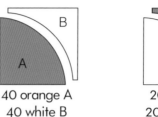

40 orange A
40 white B

20 white A
20 orange B

2. Referring to the diagram, position an A shape on a B shape, right sides together, with a ½" of B extending beyond A.

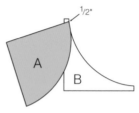

1/2"

A

B

3. Hold one shape in each hand and slowly bring the curved edges together while stitching a ¼" seam. Press seam toward A to make an AB unit. Press the unit from the front and back.

Press seam

A

B

4. Repeat with the remaining A and B shapes to make a total of 60 AB units.

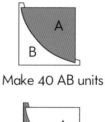

A

B

Make 40 AB units

A

B

Make 20 AB units

SQUARING UP THE AB UNITS

Square up the AB units to 6-½". Position the QCR on an AB unit with the 6-½" mark on the curved seam in the corners as shown. Leave an ⅛" from curved seam to outer edge. Trim the right and top edges of the unit. Lift the ruler and rotate the unit 180-degrees. Reposition the QCR on the unit so the previously trimmed edges are now on the 6-½" vertical and horizontal lines. Trim the right and top edges. Repeat with the remaining AB units.

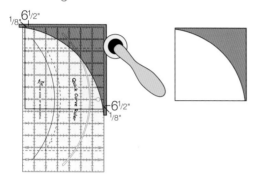

MAKING THE SIDE SECTIONS

1. Referring to the diagram, lay out 12 AB units and (4) 6-½" solid white squares in rows as shown. Sew the pieces together in rows. Press seams.

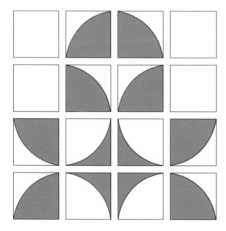

2. Sew the rows together to make a side section. Press seams. Make a total of 4 side sections.

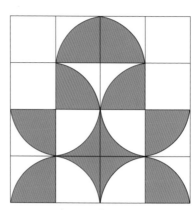

Make 4 side sections

MAKING THE CENTER SECTION

1. Referring to the diagram, lay out 12 AB units and (4) 6-½" solid white squares in rows as shown. Sew the pieces together in rows. Press seams.

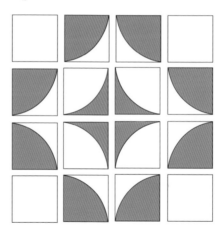

2. Sew the rows together to make the center section. Press seams.

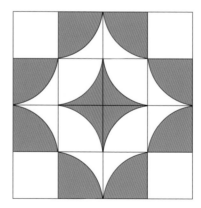

Make 1 center section

QUILT ASSEMBLY

1. Referring to the Quilt Assembly Diagram, lay out (4) 24-½" solid white squares, 4 side sections and the center section as shown.

2. Sew the pieces together in rows. Press seams. Sew the rows together to complete the quilt center. Press seams.

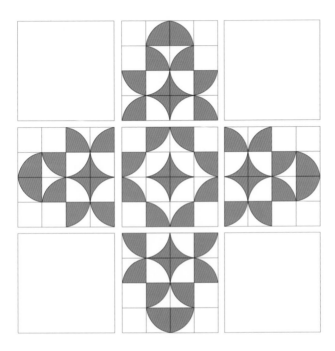

Quilt Assembly Diagram

3. Sew 1-½" x 72-½" borders to opposite sides of the quilt center. Press seams toward border.

4. Sew 1-½" x 74-½" borders to the top and bottom of the quilt center. Press seams toward border to complete the quilt top.

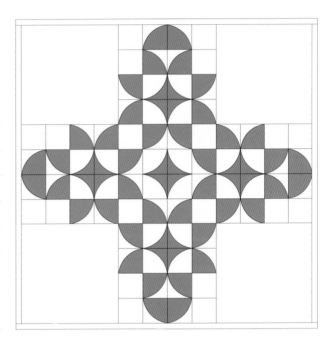

FINISHING THE QUILT

1. Layer the quilt top, batting and backing together. Quilt as desired.

2. Sew the (8) 2-½" x WOF binding strips together to make one continuous strip. Press the strip in half lengthwise and sew the binding strip to the raw edge of the quilt top. Fold binding over raw edges and hand stitch in place on back of quilt.

The fabric choice in Dragon Glass led to the design. I wanted to cut this fabric line in larger pieces so the play on color and shapes could be appreciated. The rich colors remind me of a dragon hoarding its jewels.

Jenny

Finished size: 48" x 58"

Dragon Glass Quilt

MATERIALS

(16) fat quarters assorted prints
¼ yard solid tan fabric
½ yard binding fabric
3-¼ yards backing fabric
Quick Curve Ruler© (QCR)

GENERAL CUTTING INSTRUCTIONS

From *each* assorted print fat quarter, cut as shown:

(4) 7-½" squares

(2) 3-½" squares

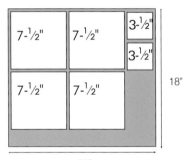

From solid tan fabric, cut:
(3) 2-½" x WOF strips. Sew the strips together
    end to end and cut:
      (2) 2-½" x 48-½" border strips

From binding fabric, cut:
(6) 2-½" x WOF binding strips

WOF = width of fabric
Read through Using the Quick Curve Ruler©
on pages 6-9 before beginning this project.

Note: A design wall is recommended while making
this project.

CUTTING WITH QUICK CURVE RULER©

1. Stack a few 7-½" assorted print squares, right
   sides up. Measure and mark ½" on adjacent sides
   as shown.

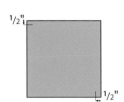

2. Position the QCR on the squares with the ruler's
   curve cut out on the ½" marks. Cut in the curve
   cut out with a rotary cutter to make A and B shapes
   as shown.

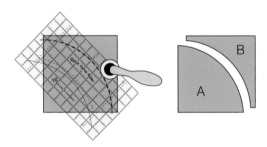

3. Repeat with the remaining 7-½" assorted print
   squares to make 64 A and 64 B shapes.

Make 64 print A
and B shapes

COLOR LAYOUT DESIGN FOR DRAGON GLASS BLOCKS

Using the Quilt Layout Diagram as a guide, lay out matching A and B shapes on a design wall to create the dragon glass blocks.

Note: The top, bottom and sides are made up of half dragon glass blocks.

Once you are happy with the color layout design, sew the A and B pieces together. Refer to **Piecing the Curves**.

PIECING THE CURVES

1. Referring to your color layout design, sew the A and B shapes together one row at a time.

2. Referring to the diagram, position an A shape on a B shape, right sides together, with a ½" of B extending beyond A.

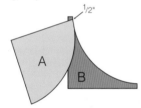

3. Hold one shape in each hand and slowly bring the curved edges together while stitching a ¼" seam. Press seam toward A to make an AB unit. Press the unit from the front and back.

Press seam

4. Repeat with the remaining A and B shapes to make a total of 64 AB units.

Make 64

SQUARING UP THE AB UNITS

Keeping the units within each row, square up the AB units one at a time to 6-½". Position the QCR on an AB unit with the 6-½" mark on the curved seam in the corners as shown. Leave an ⅛" from curved seam to outer edge. Trim the right and top edges of the unit. Lift the ruler and rotate the unit 180-degrees. Reposition the QCR on the unit so the previously trimmed edges are now on the 6-½" vertical and horizontal lines. Trim the right and top edges. Repeat with the remaining AB units.

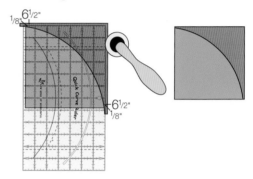

Note: Place the AB units back into their rows after squaring each one up.

QUILT ASSEMBLY

Note: Leave the units in rows on your design wall until you are ready to sew the units into rows.

1. Sew the AB units together in rows. Press seams. Sew the rows together to complete the quilt center. Press seams.

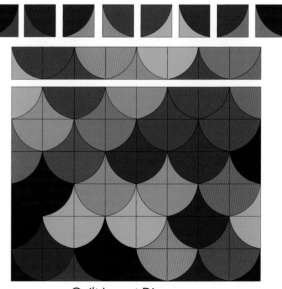

Quilt Layout Diagram

2. Sew 2-$\frac{1}{2}$" x 48-$\frac{1}{2}$" tan border strips to the top and bottom of the quilt center. Press.

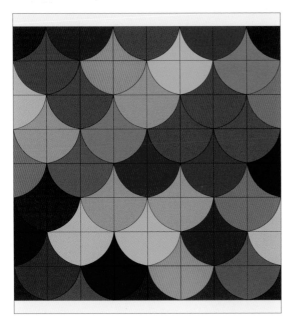

3. Lay out (16) 3-$\frac{1}{2}$" squares in a row. Sew the squares together to make a pieced row. Make 2 pieced rows.

Make 2 pieced rows

4. Sew the pieced rows to the top and bottom of the quilt center. Press to complete the quilt top.

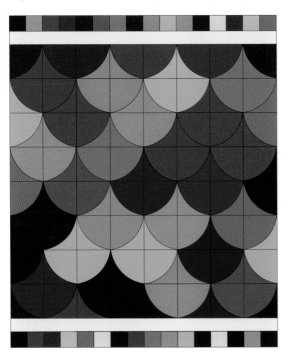

FINISHING THE QUILT

1. Layer the quilt top, batting and backing together. Quilt as desired.

2. Sew the (6) 2-$\frac{1}{2}$" x WOF binding strips together to make one continuous strip. Press the strip in half lengthwise and sew the binding strip to the raw edge of the quilt top. Fold binding over raw edges and hand stitch in place on back of quilt.

Everything about this quilt screams Moody Blues—the layout, the color and the fabric.
The variation of blues made this quilt easy to name.

Sherilyn

Finished size: 79" x 79"

Moody Blues Quilt

MATERIALS

(9) ½ yard assorted blue prints
3-¼ yards solid white fabric
½ yard solid navy fabric
1-¼ yards solid gray fabric
1 yard solid citrine fabric
¼ yard solid aqua fabric
7 yards backing fabric
⅔ yard binding fabric
Quick Curve Ruler© (QCR)

WOF = width of fabric
Read through Using the Quick Curve Ruler©
on pages 6-9 before beginning this project.

GENERAL CUTTING INSTRUCTIONS

From *each* assorted blue print cut:
(4) 7-½" squares

(2) 7" x 12" pieces

From solid white fabric cut:
(15) 7-½" x WOF strips. From the strips, cut:
    (72) 7-½" squares

From solid navy fabric, cut:
(4) 4" x WOF strips. From the strips, cut:
    (36) 4" squares

(4) 2" cornerstone squares

From solid gray fabric, cut:
(2) 8" x WOF strips. From the strips, cut:
    (10) 8" squares. Cut each in half diagonally
    to make 20 triangles

(3) 2" x WOF strips. From the strips, cut:
    (8) 2" x 12-½" sashing strips

(8) 2-½" x WOF strips. Sew the strips together
    end to end and cut:
    (2) 2-½" x 75-½" border strips
    (2) 2-½" x 79-½" border strips

From solid citrine fabric, cut:
(2) 8" x WOF strips. From the strips, cut:
    (8) 8" squares. Cut each in half diagonally to
    make 16 triangles

(6) 2" x WOF strips. From the strips, cut:
    (4) 2" x 24-½" sashing strips
    (8) 2" x 12-½" sashing strips

From solid aqua fabric, cut:
(3) 2-½" x WOF strips. From the strips, cut:
    (36) 2-½" squares

From binding fabric, cut:
(9) 2-½" x WOF binding strips

CUTTING WITH QUICK CURVE RULER©

1. Stack a few 7-½" assorted blue print squares, right sides up. Measure and mark ½" on adjacent sides as shown.

2. Position the QCR on the squares with the ruler's curve cut out on the ½" marks. Cut in the curve cut out with a rotary cutter to make A and B shapes as shown.

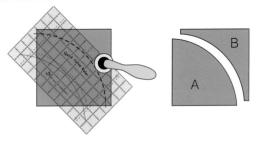

3. Repeat with the remaining 7-½" assorted blue print and solid white squares. You should have a total of 36 assorted blue print A and B shapes and 72 white A and B shapes.

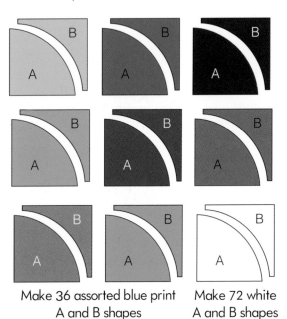

Make 36 assorted blue print A and B shapes   Make 72 white A and B shapes

4. Stack a few 8" solid gray and citrine triangles, right sides up. Measure in ½" on both points and trim as shown.

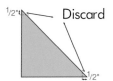

Discard

5. Position the QCR on the triangles with the ruler's curve cut out on the ½" marks. Cut in the curve cut out with a rotary cutter to make B shapes as shown.

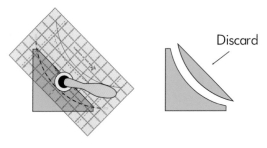

Discard

6. Repeat with the remaining 8" solid gray and citrine triangles to make a total of 16 citrine and 20 solid gray B shapes.

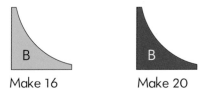

Make 16   Make 20

7. Stack a few 7" x 12" assorted blue print pieces. Measure and mark 7" on each long edge as shown.

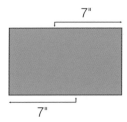

8. Position the QCR on the fabric with the ruler's curve cut out on the 7" mark and opposite corner. Cut in the curve cut out to make an A shape as shown.

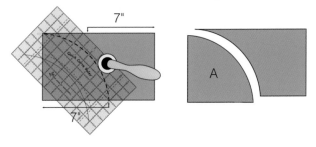

9. In the same manner, position the QCR on the remaining 7" mark and cut to make another A shape. Discard small piece in center. Repeat with the remaining 7" x 12" assorted blue print pieces to make a total of 36 blue print A shapes.

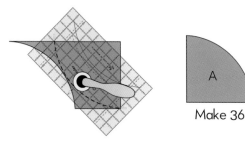

Make 36

PIECING THE CURVES

1. Separate the A and B shapes into sets as shown.

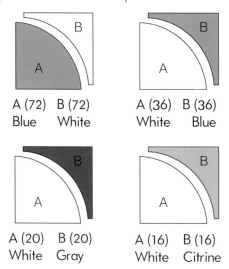

A (72) B (72)
Blue   White

A (36) B (36)
White   Blue

A (20) B (20)
White   Gray

A (16) B (16)
White   Citrine

2. Referring to the diagram, position a blue print A shape on a white B shape, right sides together, with a ½" of B extending beyond A.

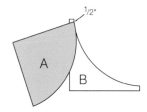

3. Hold one shape in each hand and slowly bring the curved edges together while stitching a ¼" seam. Press seam toward A to make an AB unit. Press the unit from the front and back.

Press seam

4. Repeat with the remaining A and B shapes.

SQUARING UP THE AB UNITS

Square up the AB units to 6-½". Position the QCR on an AB unit with the 6-½" mark on the curved seam in the corners as shown. Leave an ⅛" from curved seam to outer edge. Trim the right and top edges of the unit. Lift the ruler and rotate the unit 180-degrees. Reposition the QCR on the unit so the previously trimmed edges are now on the 6-½" vertical and horizontal lines. Trim the right and top edges. Repeat with the remaining AB units.

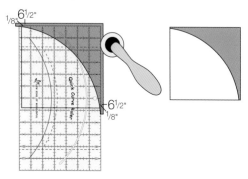

MAKING THE CENTER UNITS

1. Draw a diagonal line on the wrong side of the 4" solid navy squares and 2-½" solid aqua squares as shown.

2. Layer a marked 4" solid navy square on a white/blue AB unit, right sides together, with the marked square on the corner of the white piece. Stitch on the drawn line.

3. Trim ¼" past the stitched line. Press open to make a C unit.

4. Layer a marked 2-½" solid aqua square on the C unit, right sides together, with the marked square on the corner of the solid navy piece. Stitch on the drawn line.

5. Trim ¼" past the stitched line. Press open to make a center unit. Make a total of 36 center units.

Make 36

MAKING THE MOODY BLUES BLOCK

Note: Separate the solid white/blue AB units into 9 matching sets. Determine the color layout for the blocks.

CORNER BLOCKS

1. Lay out 8 blue/white AB units, 4 center units, 3 white/gray AB units and 1 white/citrine AB unit in 4 rows as shown.

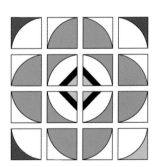

2. Sew the units together in rows. Press seams. Sew the rows together to make a corner block. Press seams. Make a total of 4 corner blocks.

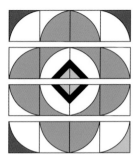 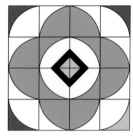

Make 4 corner blocks

SIDE CENTER BLOCKS

1. Lay out 8 blue/white AB units, 4 center units, 2 white/gray AB units and 2 white/citrine AB units in 4 rows as shown.

2. Sew the units together in rows. Press seams. Sew the rows together to make a side center block. Press seams. Make a total of 4 side center blocks.

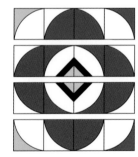 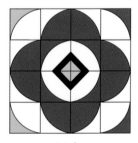

Make 4
side center blocks

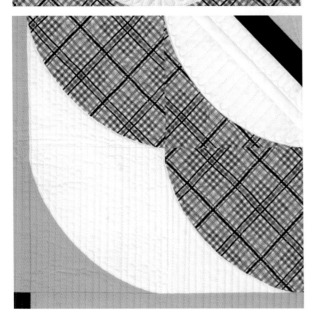

CENTER BLOCK

1. Lay out 8 blue/white AB units, 4 center units and 4 white/citrine AB unit in 4 rows as shown.

2. Sew the units together in rows. Press seams. Sew the rows together to make a center block. Press seams.

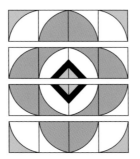
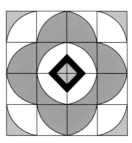

Make 1 center block

MAKING THE SASHING STRIPS

Sew the 2" x 12-½" solid gray and citrine sashing pieces together as shown to make a gray/citrine sashing strip. Press seams. Make a total of (8) gray/citrine sashing strips.

Make 8

QUILT ASSEMBLY

1. Referring to the Quilt Assembly Diagram, lay out the corner, side center and center blocks, gray/citrine sashing strips, navy cornerstones and 2" x 24-½" citrine sashing strips in rows as shown.

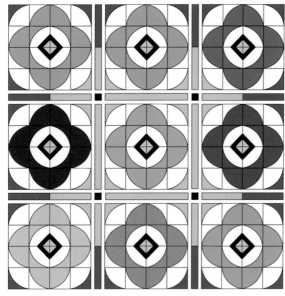

Quilt Assembly Diagram

2. Sew the pieces together in rows. Press seams toward sashing.

3. Sew the rows together to complete the quilt center. Press seams toward sashing.

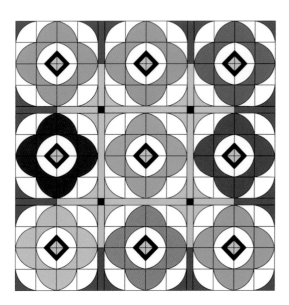

4. Sew 2-½" x 75-½" solid gray border strips to opposite sides of the quilt center. Press seams toward border strips.

5. Sew 2-½" x 79-½" solid gray border strips to the top and bottom of the quilt center. Press seams toward border strips.

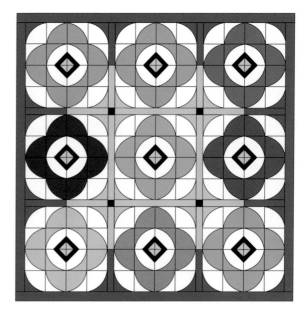

FINISHING THE QUILT

1. Layer the quilt top, batting and backing together. Quilt as desired.

2. Sew the (9) 2-½" x WOF binding strips together to make one continuous strip. Press the strip in half lengthwise and sew the binding strip to the raw edge of the quilt top. Fold binding over raw edges and hand stitch in place on back of quilt.

The bold black and white colors in Lucky show off larger secondary designs when the blocks are set on-point. There is also plenty of space for custom quilting, which was just as fun to design as the quilt itself.

Helen

Finished size: 57" x 57"

Lucky Quilt

MATERIALS

1-1/8 yards solid black fabric
1/2 yard solid green fabric
2-2/3 yards white background fabric
4 yards backing fabric
1/2 yard binding fabric
Quick Curve Ruler© (QCR)

GENERAL CUTTING INSTRUCTIONS

From solid black fabric, cut:

(3) 8" x WOF strips. From the strips, cut:
    (14) 8" squares. Cut each in half diagonally
    to make 28 triangles

(2) 5" x WOF strips. From the strips, cut:
    (12) 5" squares

(1) 2" x WOF strip. From the strip, cut:
    (9) 2" squares

From solid green fabric, cut:

(1) 8" x WOF strip. From the strip, cut:
    (4) 8" squares. Cut each in half diagonally to
    make 8 triangles

(1) 5" x WOF strip. From the strip, cut:
    (4) 5" squares

From white background fabric, cut:

(6) 7" x WOF strips. From the strips, cut:
    (18) 7"x 12" pieces

(3) 5" x WOF strips. From the strips, cut:
    (20) 5" squares

(2) 6-1/2" x WOF strips. From the strips, cut:
    (36) 2" x 6-1/2" pieces

(2) 20-3/8" squares. Cut
    each in half twice on the
    diagonal to make 8 side
    setting triangles

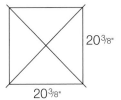

(2) 10-1/2" squares. Cut each in half diagonally
    to make 4 corner setting triangles.

From binding fabric, cut:
(6) 2-1/2" x WOF binding strips

WOF = width of fabric
Read through *Using the Quick Curve Ruler©*
on pages 6-9 before beginning this project.

CUTTING WITH QUICK CURVE RULER©

1. Stack a few 8" solid black triangles, right sides up. Measure in ½" on both points and trim as shown.

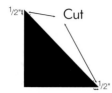

2. Position the QCR on the triangles with the ruler's curve cut out on the ½" marks. Cut in the curve cut out with a rotary cutter to make B shapes as shown.

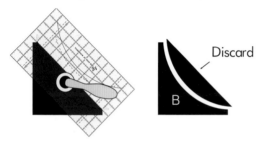

3. Repeat with the remaining 8" solid black and green triangles to make a total of 28 black and 8 green B shapes.

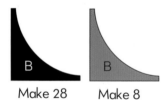

Make 28   Make 8

4. Stack a few 7" x 12" white background pieces, right sides up. Measure and mark 7" on each long edge as shown.

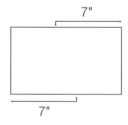

5. Position the QCR on the fabric with the ruler's curve cut out on the 7" mark and opposite corner. Cut in the curve cut out to make an A shape as shown.

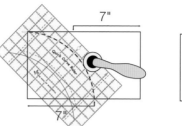
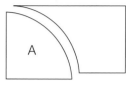

6. In the same manner, position the QCR on the remaining 7" mark and cut to make another A shape. Discard small piece in center. Repeat with the remaining 7" x 12" white background pieces to make a total of 36 white A shapes.

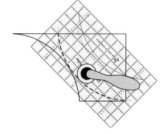
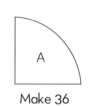

Make 36

PIECING THE CURVES

1. Separate the A and B shapes into sets as shown.

A (28) B (28)   A (8)   B (8)
White   Black   White   Green

2. Referring to the diagram, position an A shape on a B shape, right sides together, with a ½" of B extending beyond A.

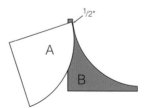

3. Hold one shape in each hand and slowly bring the curved edges together while stitching a ¼" seam. Press seam toward A to make an AB unit. Press the unit from the front and back.

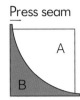

Press seam

4. Repeat with the remaining A and B shapes to make a total of 28 white/black and 8 white/green AB units.

Make 28   Make 8

SQUARING UP THE AB UNITS

Square up the AB units to 6-½". Position the QCR on an AB unit with the 6-½" mark on the curved seam in the corners as shown. Leave an ⅛" from curved seam to outer edge. Trim the right and top edges of the unit. Lift the ruler and rotate the unit 180-degrees. Reposition the QCR on the unit so the previously trimmed edges are now on the 6-½" vertical and horizontal lines. Trim the right and top edges. Repeat with the remaining AB units.

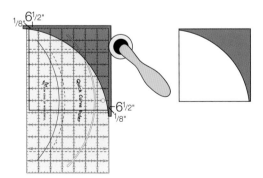

MAKING THE BLOCKS

1. Lay out 4 white/black AB units, (4) 2" x 6-½" white pieces and (1) black 2" square in 3 rows as shown.

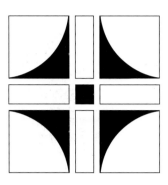

2. Sew the pieces together in rows. Press seams. Sew the rows together to make a black block. Press seams. Make a total of 4 black blocks.

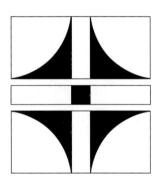

Make 4

3. Repeat steps 1 and 2 to make 1 green block and 4 black/green blocks as shown.

Make 1   Make 4

4. Lay out 5 white, 3 black and 1 green 5" squares in 3 rows as shown.

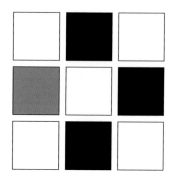

5. Sew the pieces together in rows. Press seams. Sew the rows together to make a nine-patch block. Press seams. Make a total of 4 nine-patch blocks.

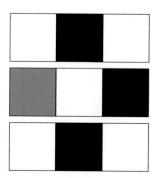 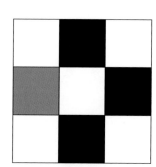

Make 4

QUILT ASSEMBLY

1. Referring to the Quilt Assembly Diagram, lay out the blocks and setting triangles in diagonal rows as shown.

Quilt Assembly Diagram

2. Sew the blocks and side setting triangles together in diagonal rows. Press the seams in each row in alternating directions.

3. Sew a corner setting triangle to each corner to complete the quilt top.

4. Square up the quilt top leaving a ¼" beyond the block points.

FINISHING THE QUILT

1. Layer the quilt top, batting and backing together. Quilt as desired.

2. Sew the (6) 2-½" x WOF binding strips together to make one continuous strip. Press the strip in half lengthwise and sew the binding strip to the raw edge of the quilt top. Fold binding over raw edges and hand stitch in place on back of quilt.

Parasail is a team favorite. When the blocks are sewn together a secondary oval design appears. It's mesmerizing, fun and comforting, all wrapped up into one appealing design.

Sherilyn

Finished size: 84" x 84"

Parasail Quilt

MATERIALS

1 yard solid green fabric
1 yard solid navy fabric
1 yard solid aqua fabric
1 yard solid gray fabric
2/3 yard solid red fabric
5 yards solid white background fabric
9 fat eighths assorted prints
3/4 yard binding fabric
8 yards backing fabric
Quick Curve Ruler© (QCR)

GENERAL CUTTING INSTRUCTIONS

Note: Cut all fabrics in the order given.

From *each* solid green, navy, aqua and gray fabric, cut:

(1) 8" x WOF strip. From the strip, cut:
  (4) 8" squares. Cut each in half diagonally to make 8 triangles from each color
  From remainder of 8" strip, cut:
  (1) 7-1/2" square

(3) 7-1/2" x WOF strips. From the strips, cut:
  (15) 7-1/2" squares

From solid red fabric, cut:

(1) 8" x WOF strip. From the strip, cut:
  (2) 8" squares. Cut each in half diagonally to make a total of 4 triangles

(2) 7-1/2" x WOF strips. From the strips, cut:
  (8) 7-1/2" squares

From solid white background fabric, cut:

(12) 7" x WOF strips. From the strips, cut:
  (36) 7" x 12" pieces

(4) 8" x WOF strips. From the strips, cut:
  (18) 8" squares. Cut each in half diagonally to make a total of 36 triangles

(8) 2-1/2" x WOF strips. Sew strips together end to end and cut:
  (6) 2-1/2" x 24-1/2" sashing strips
  (2) 2-1/2" x 76-1/2" sashing strips

(9) 4-1/2" x WOF strips. Sew strips together end to end and cut:
  (2) 4-1/2" x 76-1/2" border strips
  (2) 4-1/2" x 84-1/2" border strips

 From each assorted print fat eighth, cut:

(4) 4" squares

(4) 2-1/2" squares

From binding fabric, cut:
(9) 2-1/2" x WOF binding strips

WOF = width of fabric
Read through Using the Quick Curve Ruler©
on pages 6-9 before beginning this project.

CUTTING WITH QUICK CURVE RULER©

1. Stack a few 7-½" solid fabric squares, right sides up. Measure and mark ½" on adjacent sides as shown.

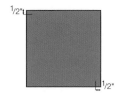

2. Position the QCR on the fabric with the ruler's curve cut out on the ½" marks. Cut in the curve cut out with a rotary cutter to make A and B shapes as shown.

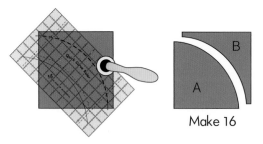

Make 16

3. Repeat with the remaining 7-½" solid fabric squares to make a total of 72 solid A and B shapes.

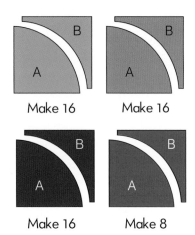

Make 16   Make 16

Make 16   Make 8

4. Stack a few 8" solid fabric triangles together, right sides up. Measure in ½" on both points and trim as shown.

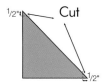

Cut

5. Position the QCR on the triangles with the curve cut out over the points as shown. Using a rotary cutter, cut in the curve cut out to make a B shape. Discard the small pieces. Repeat with the remaining 8" solid fabric triangles to make a total of 72 solid B shapes.

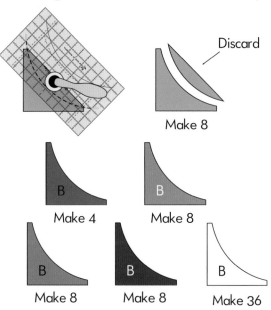

Discard

Make 8

B Make 4   B Make 8

B Make 8   B Make 8   B Make 36

6. Stack a few 7" x 12" solid white background pieces, right sides up. Measure and mark 7" on each long edge as shown.

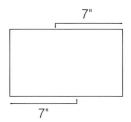

7"

7"

7. Position the QCR on the fabric with the ruler's curve cut out on the 7" mark and opposite corner. Cut in the curve cut out to make an A shape as shown.

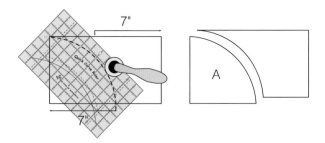

7"

7"

A

8. In the same manner, position the QCR on the remaining 7" mark and cut to make another A shape. Discard small piece in center. Repeat with the remaining 7" x 12" solid white background pieces to make a total of 72 A shapes.

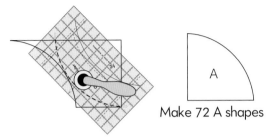

Make 72 A shapes

Note: You should now have the following shapes in the colors shown.

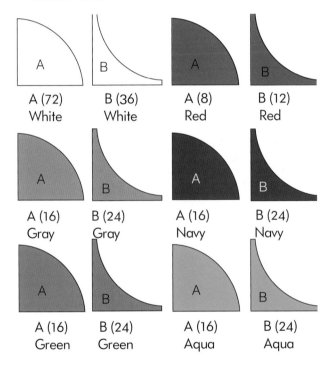

A (72) White   B (36) White   A (8) Red   B (12) Red

A (16) Gray   B (24) Gray   A (16) Navy   B (24) Navy

A (16) Green   B (24) Green   A (16) Aqua   B (24) Aqua

PIECING THE CURVES

1. Each parasail block is made up of a different fabric color combination. Referring to the quilt photo on page 66, separate the A and B shapes into 9 sets to represent the 9 parasail blocks.

For example, the red parasail block uses the following shapes and colors: 8 solid red A, 8 solid red B, 8 solid white A, 4 solid white B and 4 solid gray B.

Sew the following sets together.

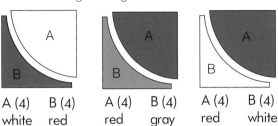

A (4) white   B (4) red   A (4) red   B (4) gray   A (4) red   B (4) white

2. Referring to the diagram, position an A shape on a B shape, right sides together, with a ½" of B extending beyond A.

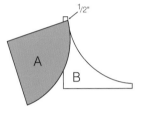

3. Hold one shape in each hand and slowly bring the curved edges together while stitching a ¼" seam. Press seam toward A to make an AB unit. Press the unit from the front and back.

Press seam

4. Repeat to make a total of 9 parasail block sets. Each set will have 16 AB units.

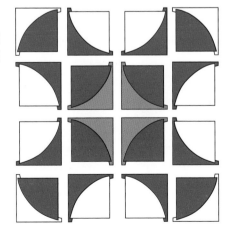

SQUARING UP THE AB UNITS

Square up the AB units to 6-½". Position the QCR on an AB unit with the 6-½" mark on the curved seam in the corners as shown. Leave an ⅛" from curved seam to outer edge. Trim the right and top edges of the unit. Lift the ruler and rotate the unit 180-degrees. Reposition the QCR on the unit so the previously trimmed edges are now on the 6-½" vertical and horizontal lines. Trim the right and top edges. Repeat with the remaining AB units.

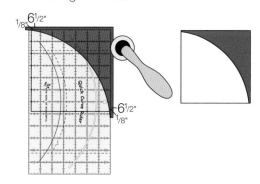

PIECING ACCENT TRIANGLES AND CENTERS

1. Lay out one parasail block set as shown.

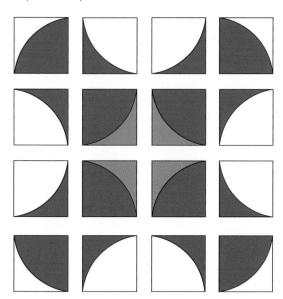

2. Draw a line on the wrong side of the 4" and 2-½" assorted print squares as shown.

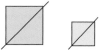

3. Referring to the diagram, layer a marked 4" square on the corner of an AB unit, right sides together, as shown. Stitch on the drawn line.

4. Trim ¼" past the stitched line. Press open to make a C unit. Make 8 C units.

Make 8 C units

5. Referring to the diagram, layer a marked 2-½" square on the corner of a C unit, right sides together, as shown. Stitch on the drawn line.

6. Trim ¼" past the stitched line. Press open to make a D unit. Make 4 D units.

Make 4 D units

7. Repeat with the remaining parasail block sets.

MAKING THE PARASAIL BLOCKS

1. Lay out 8 AB units, 4 C units and 4 D units for one parasail block as shown.

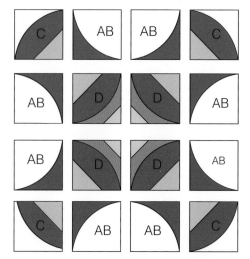

2. Sew the units together in rows. Sew the rows together to make a parasail block. Press seams open to reduce bulk. The block should measure 24-½" square. Repeat with various color layouts for remaining 8 parasail blocks. Make a total of 9 parasail blocks.

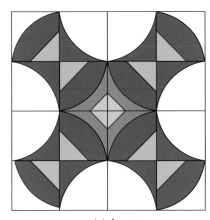

Make 9

QUILT ASSEMBLY

1. Referring to the Quilt Assembly Diagram, lay out the parasail blocks, 2-½" x 24-½" solid white sashing strips and 2-½" x 76-½" solid white sashing strips in rows as shown.

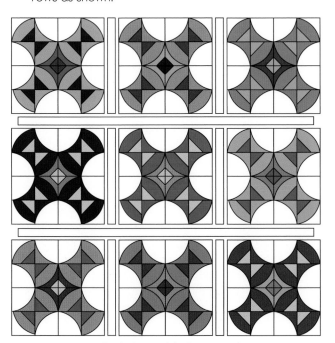

Quilt Assembly Diagram

2. Sew the blocks and 2-½" x 24-½" sashing strips together in 3 rows. Press seams toward sashing.

3. Sew the rows and 2-½" x 76-½" sashing strips together to complete the quilt center. Press seams toward sashing.

4. Sew 4-½" x 76-½" solid white border strips to the top and bottom of the quilt center. Press seams toward border strips.

5. Sew 4-½" x 84-½" solid white border strips to opposite sides of the quilt center. Press seams toward border strips to complete the quilt top.

FINISHING THE QUILT

1. Layer the quilt top, batting and backing together. Quilt as desired.

2. Sew the (9) 2-½" x WOF binding strips together to make one continuous strip. Press the strip in half lengthwise and sew the binding strip to the raw edge of the quilt top. Fold binding over raw edges and hand stitch in place on back of quilt.

71

Green is my favorite color, my birthstone is an emerald and my middle name is Gardner. All of this suggests I should be good at growing all things green. Sadly, that is not the case. I am, however, great at buying green fabric and designing green vines. Needless to say, all the greens in Green Smoothie came from my stash.

Helen

Finished size: 82" x 86"

Green Smoothie Quilt

MATERIALS

(15) fat quarters assorted green prints
(8) fat quarters assorted blue prints
$\frac{1}{3}$ yard solid green fabric
$\frac{1}{3}$ yard solid light green fabric
$\frac{1}{4}$ yard solid dark green fabric
$\frac{1}{4}$ yard solid sage green fabric
4-$\frac{1}{2}$ yards neutral background fabric
1 yard neutral sashing fabric
$\frac{1}{3}$ yard gray fabric
$\frac{3}{4}$ yard binding fabric
8 yards backing fabric
Quick Curve Ruler© (QCR)

GENERAL CUTTING INSTRUCTIONS

Note: Refer to diagram before cutting strips.

 From *each* assorted green print fat quarter, cut:
(11) 2-$\frac{1}{4}$" x 13" strips for a total of 165 strips. You will use 160.

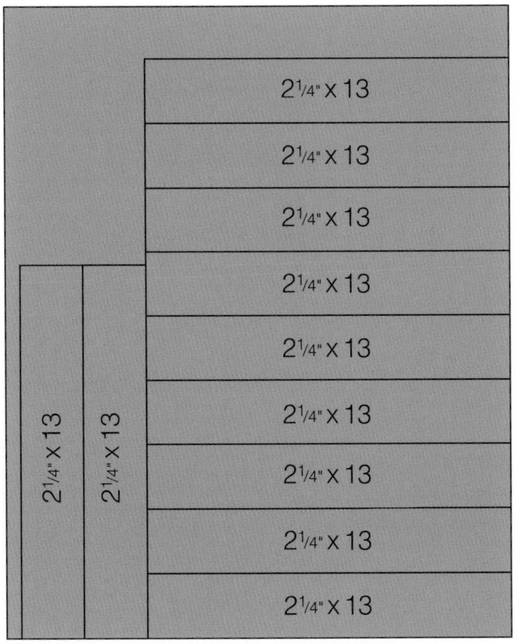

2¼" x 13	
2¼" x 13	
2¼" x 13	
2¼" x 13	2¼" x 13
2¼" x 13	
2¼" x 13	
2¼" x 13	
2¼" x 13	
2¼" x 13	

 From *each* assorted blue print fat quarter, cut:
(11) 2-$\frac{1}{4}$" x 13" strips for a total of 88 strips. You will use 80.

From solid green fabric, cut:
(4) 7" x 12" pieces

From solid light green fabric, cut:
(4) 7" x 12" pieces

From solid dark green fabric, cut:
(2) 7" x 12" pieces

From solid sage green fabric, cut:
(2) 7" x 12" pieces

From neutral background fabric, cut:
(15) 8" x WOF strips. From the strips, cut:
    (72) 8" squares. Cut each in half diagonally
    for a total of 144 triangles

(3) 12-$\frac{1}{2}$" x WOF strips. From the strips, cut:
    (66) 1-$\frac{1}{2}$" x 12-$\frac{1}{2}$" background strips

From neutral sashing fabric, cut:
(13) 2-$\frac{1}{2}$" x WOF strips. Sew strips together
    end to end and cut:
    (4) 2-$\frac{1}{2}$" x 83-$\frac{1}{2}$" sashing strips
    (2) 2-$\frac{1}{2}$" x 82" sashing strips

From gray fabric, cut:
(7) 1-$\frac{1}{2}$" x WOF. Sew strips together
    end to end and cut:
    (3) 1-$\frac{1}{2}$" x 83-$\frac{1}{2}$" stems

From binding fabric, cut:
(9) 2-$\frac{1}{2}$" x WOF binding strips

WOF = width of fabric
Read through Using the Quick Curve Ruler©
on pages 6-9 before beginning this project.

MAKING THE STRIP SETS

1. Select 4 assorted green 2-¼" x 13" strips. Sew the strips together to make a strip set. Press seams in one direction. Square the strip set to 7" x 12". Repeat to make 40 assorted green strip sets.

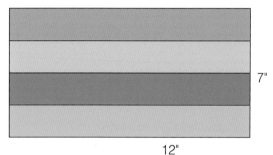

7"

12"
Make 40

2. Select 4 assorted blue 2-¼" x 13" strips. Sew the strips together to make a strip set. Press seams in one direction. Square the strip set to 7" x 12". Repeat to make 20 assorted blue strip sets.

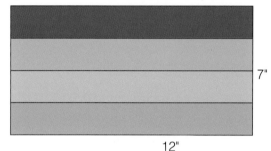

7"

12"
Make 20

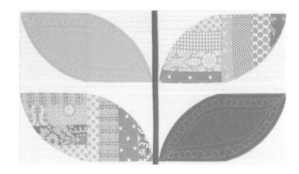

CUTTING WITH QUICK CURVE RULER©

1. Stack 2 assorted green strip sets, **right sides together**. Measure and mark 7" on each long edge as shown.

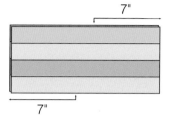

7"

7"

2. Position the QCR on the fabric with the ruler's curve cut out on the 7" mark and opposite corner. Cut in the curve cut out to make an A shape as shown.

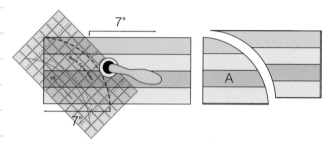

7"

7"

A

3. In the same manner, position the QCR on the remaining 7" mark and cut to make another A shape. Discard small piece in center. Repeat with the remaining 7" x 12" green and blue strip sets to make 80 green A shapes and 40 blue A shapes.

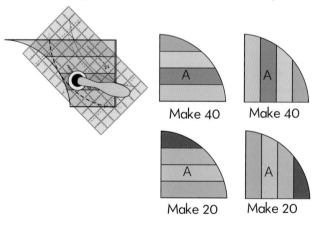

Make 40   Make 40

Make 20   Make 20

4. Repeat steps with all solid green 7" x 12" pieces for a total of 24 green fabric A shapes.

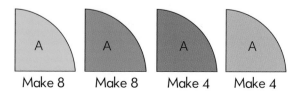

Make 8   Make 8   Make 4   Make 4

5. Stack a few 8" neutral background triangles, right sides up. Measure in $\frac{1}{2}$" on both points and trim as shown.

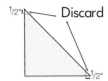

6. Position the QCR on the fabric with the ruler's curve cut out on the $\frac{1}{2}$" marks. Cut in the curve cut out with a rotary cutter to make B shapes as shown.

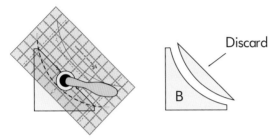

7. Repeat with the remaining 8" neutral background triangles to make a total of 144 B shapes.

Make 144

PIECING THE CURVES

1. Referring to the diagram, position an A shape on a B shape, right sides together, with a $\frac{1}{2}$" of B extending beyond A.

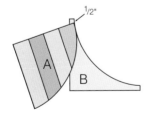

2. Hold one shape in each hand and slowly bring the curved edges together while stitching a $\frac{1}{4}$" seam. Press seam toward A to make an AB unit. Press the unit from the front and back.

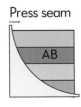

Press seam

3. Repeat with the remaining A and B shapes to make a total of 120 AB strip units and 24 AB solid units.

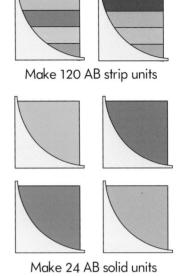

Make 120 AB strip units

Make 24 AB solid units

SQUARING UP THE AB UNITS

Square up the AB units to 6-$\frac{1}{2}$". Position the QCR on an AB unit with the 6-$\frac{1}{2}$" mark on the curved seam in the corners as shown. Leave an $\frac{1}{8}$" from curved seam to outer edge. Trim the right and top edges of the unit. Lift the ruler and rotate the unit 180-degrees. Reposition the QCR on the unit so the previously trimmed edges are now on the 6-$\frac{1}{2}$" vertical and horizontal lines. Trim the right and top edges. Repeat with the remaining AB units.

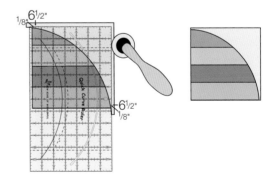

MAKING THE LEAF UNITS

1. Lay out 2 green AB strip units, alternating the direction of the strips. Sew the units together as shown to make a green leaf unit. The leaf unit should measure 6-½" x 12-½".

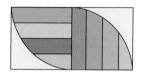

2. Referring to the diagram, repeat to make a total of 20 left green leaf units and 20 right green leaf units.

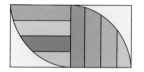 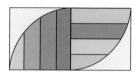

Make 20 left and 20 right green leaf units

3. In the same manner, make 10 left blue leaf units and 10 right blue leaf units.

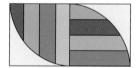 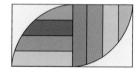

Make 10 left and 10 right blue leaf units

4. Repeat steps to make 6 left solid leaf units and 6 right solid leaf units.

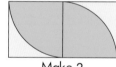
Make 2

Make 2

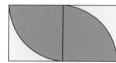
Make 2

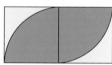
Make 2

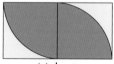
Make 1

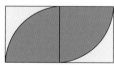
Make 1

Make 1

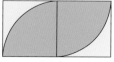
Make 1

QUILT ASSEMBLY

1. Referring to the quilt photo on page 78 and Quilt Row Assembly Diagram, lay out left and right green and blue leaf units, left and right solid leaf units and 1-½" x 12-½" background strips in 6 vertical rows as shown. There are 12 leaf units and 11 background strips in each row. Alternate the pieced leaves and solid leaf units as desired.

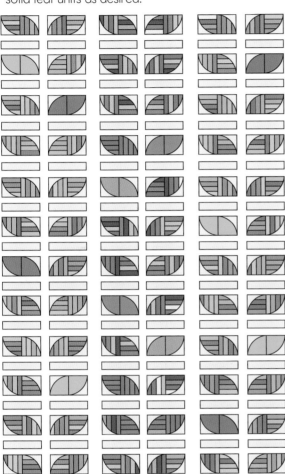

Quilt Row Assembly Diagram

2. Sew the pieces together in vertical rows. Press seams toward background strips. You will have 3 left leaf rows and 3 right leaf rows. Each row should measure approximately 12-½" x 83-½".

3. Sew a left and right leaf row to opposite sides of a 1-½" x 83-½" gray stem. Press seams toward the stem to make a leaf column. Take care to ensure the leaf unit seams match on either side of the stem. Repeat to make a total of 3 leaf columns.

4. Referring to the diagram, lay out the leaf columns and 2-½" x 83-½" neutral sashing strips as shown.

5. Sew the pieces together. Press seams toward the sashing strips to complete the quilt center.

6. Sew the 2-½" x 82" neutral sashing strip to the top and bottom of the quilt center. Press seams toward the sashing strips.

FINISHING THE QUILT

1. Layer the quilt top, batting and backing together. Quilt as desired.

2. Sew the (9) 2-½" x WOF binding strips together to make one continuous strip. Press the strip in half lengthwise and sew the binding strip to the raw edge of the quilt top. Fold binding over raw edges and hand stitch in place on back of quilt.

Quilting Suggestions

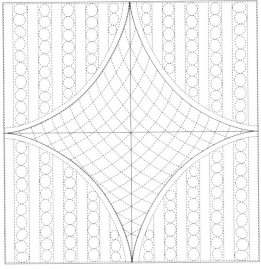

Summer Citrus Runner

Candy Blossoms Quilt

Contempo Twist Quilt

Gaggle Battle Quilt

Mod Dash Quilt

Moroccan Vibe Quilt

Quilting Suggestions

Persimmon Quilt

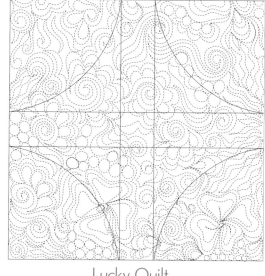

Lucky Quilt

Dragon Glass Quilt

Parasail Quilt

Moody Blues Quilt

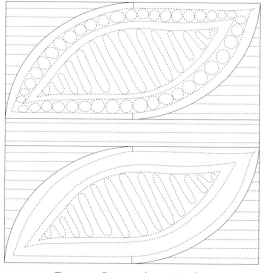

Green Smoothie Quilt